How To
BUILD
Your Network Marketing
UTILITIES
Business
FAST

KEITH & TOM "BIG AL" SCHREITER

How To Build Your Network Marketing Utilities Business Fast
© 2020 by Keith & Tom "Big Al" Schreiter

Published by Fortune Network Publishing
PO Box 890084
Houston, TX 77289 USA

Telephone: +1 (281) 280-9800

BigAlBooks.com

ISBN-13: 978-1-948197-61-8

CONTENTS

Preface v

Decisions. 1

But, but … who can I talk to first? 5

How to fix "feeling nervous" when talking to prospects. 13

Step #1: Build rapport first. 17

Step #2: Ice breakers. 27

Step #3: Closing. 41

A new distributor makes it easy. 45

Step #4: Presentation. 49

The one-minute presentation. 57

The two-minute story. 71

Group presentations. 87

Where and how to find prospects. 93

And finally. 101

Thank you. 103

More Big Al Books 105

About the Authors 110

I travel the world 240+ days each year.
Let me know if you want me to stop in your
area and conduct a live Big Al training.

BigAlSeminars.com

FREE Big Al Training Audios

Magic Words for Prospecting

plus Free eBook and the Big Al Report!

BigAlBooks.com/free

PREFACE

Do we sell phone service? Electricity? Gas? Internet service? Some other essential service?

If we do, this book will be a treasure trove of ideas on how to get our prospects to become customers or distributors. We can choose which ideas fit our business, or fit our personalities.

Not every idea here will be the perfect idea for the perfect situation. Many states and countries have varying laws, and of course, our companies have varying offers. But all it takes is one good idea to change our business and our income forever.

In this book we will cover the right things to say and do for our services and for our opportunities. Remember, it is not the quantity of ideas that we learn that makes the difference. It is the quality of the ideas that we actually put into practice. So while many things here may sound good, it won't matter unless we put them to use in our business.

Utilities and essential services are intangibles. These are difficult things for our prospects to touch and feel. That is why having the right words makes a difference. The words we say can create pictures and feelings in our prospects' minds.

Let's get started right away with some great things to say and do.

DECISIONS.

We joined a career in the "decision-making" business. Our company provides the services, the billing, the website, the lawyers, the customer service departments, and do everything for our customers.

In fact, our company can do everything ... except one thing:

Get prospects to make a "yes" decision to become a customer or to join as a distributor. And that is why our company needs us.

Here is the partnership. See if it seems fair.

The company does almost everything. All we have to do is get "yes" decisions from our prospects.

Wow! This is a great partnership. Why?

Because our job is easy. Once we learn how prospects make decisions, we can build a huge business in record time. Getting new customers? No problem. Getting new team members? No problem. When we know how to get decisions, our part of this partnership will be easy.

So the obvious question is, "How do prospects make decisions?"

Well, the answer might surprise us.

Once we know how prospects make decisions, everything changes for us. We will have the precise skills to get quick decisions. This pays off, giving us a financially rewarding career.

So, let's get down to business.

This is not how people make decisions:

- They wait for lightning to strike them.

- They listen to the little voices in their heads.

- They wait for a flash of inspiration or a sign.

- 15,000 reasons for, and 14,000 reasons against.

- They sit through a 30-minute presentation, watch videos and look at PowerPoint slides, listen to testimonials, and at the end of the presentation, they carefully weigh the pros and cons, and then make a logical decision based upon the facts.

Well, this might be what others have taught us, but the reality is much different.

If we knew exactly how humans made up their minds, how much would that be worth to us?

Millions.

And that is why we should continue reading.

Here is the short story.

The science of decision-making is an enormous subject. We won't go there in this book. All we need to learn are four simple steps to get our prospects to make a decision, so we have a successful network marketing utility business.

Step #1. Build some rapport first. If our prospects don't trust us or like us, it will end badly. Nothing we can present will make much difference. Thankfully, we only have to spend a few seconds on this step to get the trust and belief we need.

Step #2. Ice breaker. Now that our prospects will listen to us, we can introduce our business into a social conversation. Many times our prospects will make their final "yes" decision here, based on how we describe our business. Yes, it can be over that quickly.

Step #3. Closing. After we give our prospects a brief hint about our business in our ice breaker, they will have some pre-existing programs in their minds. They could have a program that means they enjoy saving money. They could have a program that they deserve to earn more money. For these prospects, a "yes" decision is instant. And for others, we can prompt them to make a "yes" or "no" decision with just a phrase or two.

The above three steps might take 15 seconds. Relax. It is hard to believe now, but we will see how it works in this book.

Step #4. If the answer to Step #3 is "yes," then and only then will we give a presentation. But the presentation is after the "yes" decision, so we will only make presentations to people who want to buy or join.

And that is it. Our presentation could take as little as 15 seconds, or as long as our prospects want. In this book we will cover lots of mini-presentations that only take a few sentences.

Now, back to the short story.

We will learn these four little steps, and we will get "yes" decisions.

So get ready for more customers and team members.

But first, we need to find people to talk to!

But, but ... who can I talk to first?

Before we can follow the four conversation steps, we first need someone to talk to. So how do we get an appointment to talk to others?

Let's take a look at the three types of prospects.

First, our relatives and close friends.

There is an old saying, "Dogs know who to bite."

Our relatives and close friends can smell a salesman from a mile away. They sense desperation and an agenda. So if they are going to sense our agenda, what should our agenda be?

To try to sell them something? That might make a bad impression.

To try to help them? Now, that is going to go over well with them.

Before we talk to our close relatives and friends, let's think about our agenda. What is an agenda? It is our intention or expected outcome.

Prospects notice our body language, our micro-facial expressions, and our tone of voice. Whatever our chosen agenda, it will shine through. Our agenda will have more impact than the actual words we say.

Before we say our first words, let's establish our agenda in our minds. We should think:

1. I want to help them.

2. I will offer an "option."

3. They can decide if this option works for them now, or not.

And what will this option be?

Maybe we will offer them an opportunity to have a second income in their lives. Or, an opportunity to lower their utility bills.

But remember, we are offering an option. That means no convincing, and no high-pressure sales techniques.

Think of it like picking a coffee shop to go to. We can suggest a coffee shop to our close relatives and friends, but it is okay if they choose not to go there.

Our prospects appreciate extra options in their lives. Who wouldn't? We could say, "This is one more option for your life. You can take advantage of this option now, later, or never. But you will always have this extra option."

What happens? Our prospects sense our intention is to add one more option for their lives. This helps us avoid the skepticism and distrust that cause our prospects to hesitate.

This means no rejection and no pressure. We gift our prospects with an option. Done.

Our relatives and close friends know us well. They will instantly detect our intention.

What to say to relatives and close friends.

We have rapport and trust with these people. They have experience with us. However, we will feel guilty if these people think, "Oh, you are just trying to make money off me." Fortunately, by having "options" as our agenda, most people will sense our real intentions.

Still, we might feel hesitant to approach everyone that we know. And some people are intimidating. We have no idea how to approach them without rejection.

To solve this, we will use the comfortable/uncomfortable formula. This allows us to tell them we have an opportunity, but gives them an escape so they don't feel trapped. Here it is in action.

"Anne, I am perfectly comfortable with your decision to look at my business or not. But I was uncomfortable not asking if you wanted to look, and having you think that I didn't care."

How does Anne feel when she hears this invitation to learn about our business? She feels good. If she has an interest, she feels honored that we wanted to talk to her right away. If she doesn't have an interest, we told her that it is okay if she doesn't want to look. She doesn't feel bad. We didn't jeopardize our friendship. We don't feel guilty. And with this formula, we can approach everyone. Let's do another example.

"Paul, I am listening to an online business presentation tonight. This is a business that you can do too. I am comfortable if you want to join me tonight, or not. No problem. I just felt uncomfortable not letting you know about this business."

How does Paul feel? Good. He has options. We don't judge him or our friendship based on which option he takes.

Another example?

"Hi, Mary. I got tired of working overtime at my job for extra money, so I started a part-time business from my home. I thought it might be interesting for you also. I am comfortable if you want to take a look at it, or not. I just felt uncomfortable not letting you know about it."

With this technique of comfortable/uncomfortable, we only take the volunteers.

The volunteers are ready for action. If we press for an appointment, what does that signal? Either our prospects are skeptical of our approach, or it is not the right time for them. Both situations will burn up time and make everyone feel bad.

The comfortable/uncomfortable formula gets to the point quickly. We won't have people lingering on our "to call" list because we don't know what to say. It only takes a few minutes to sort out the relatives and close friends who are interested.

We can do the same sort of invitation for customers. Here is a quick example.

"Hey George. You get an electricity bill every month just like I do. We can save a lot of money on that bill. I am okay if you want to take advantage of this or not, but I at least wanted to let you know you could have some extra cash in your pocket every month. I didn't want you to feel like I wouldn't think of you right away."

As we can see, if we don't like using comfortable/uncomfortable, we could adjust. In this case we used the word "okay" instead, but we get the general idea.

Second group? People we know who are not relatives or close friends.

We may not have rapport with these people. They don't really know us. So, we will have to do more in our conversation to connect for an appointment.

These people won't want to meet with us just because we have a strong connection. They want a reason to meet. And this means they will want to protect their time from:

1. Salespeople.

2. Presentations about things that are not interesting to them.

We have two ways to get them interested in meeting with us.

First, we can tell them we have wonderful benefits.

Let's list a few of these benefits now:

- Lower phone bills.
- Lower electricity bills.
- More money for their children's allowances.
- A second income to pay their bills.
- A chance to work from home instead of going to work.

We could simply ask them if they wanted one of these benefits. For example, "Would you like your phone bill to be lower every month?"

It won't take long for them to say, "Sure. Let's talk." Or, they could also say, "No thanks. I will keep paying a higher bill."

Why would they want a higher bill? We don't know. But here are a few reasons they wouldn't want to meet with us:

- They had a bad experience with a pushy salesman recently.

- Their spouse yelled at them, and they have other issues on their minds.

- We don't know if their mother dropped them on their head as a child, or if something traumatic happened 30 minutes before talking to us.

- We look like their ex-girlfriend or ex-boyfriend. Nothing we can do about that.

So don't worry. This is life. Some want to take our option that improves their lives, some don't. The good news is this choice is over in seconds. And because we gave them a choice, no one is offended.

Second, we can let them know we might have a solution to their problems.

This is even more powerful. We worry about our problems all the time. Here are a few problems they might have:

- High utility bills.

- No money at the end of the month.

- Meager retirement savings.

- A soul-sucking commute to work.

- A terrible boss or unfulfilling career.

In this case our conversation would look like this:

Us: "Do you have [this problem]? Would it be okay if we could fix it?"

Here is an example:

Us: "Do you hate high phone bills?"

Prospect: "Of course."

Us: "Would it be okay if we could make them lower?"

Prospect: "Sure. When can we talk?"

Third group? People we don't know at all.

Now things are harder with this group. When they first come into contact with us, they will be thinking:

- Who is this person?
- What does this person want?
- Can I trust this person?
- Should I set up my salesmen defenses?
- Is it time to be skeptical?

This means we don't have rapport with this stranger. We will spend time in our first contact with this stranger attempting to get trust and rapport. Once we accomplish this, then we can move on to getting an appointment. Yes, we might invest two or more engagements with a stranger to create rapport first.

Some people are natural trust-builders. They can achieve rapport in seconds. Other people? We have to work harder to connect with strangers.

For now, don't worry about the strangers yet. We will learn how to create rapport with them, and then our ice breaker will pre-sell them on what we're offering.

The good news is that we will create many new friendships along the way. And yes, many of our new friends will want exactly what we offer.

How to fix "feeling nervous" when talking to prospects.

It isn't our presentation that makes us nervous.

It is our **intention** that makes us nervous.

Is our intention to sign them up, close them, or get them to be customers?

Well, that shows all over our facial expressions, our tone of voice, our body language and in the words we say. Prospects can smell pushy, self-centered salespeople a mile away.

But what if our intention is to offer them an **option**? We don't care if they take the option or not, we only care that they understand the option.

Then we neutralize our personal feelings. We accept whatever decisions our prospects make. We want what is best for them. And then what happens? We project that intention and our prospects relax. Now our conversations become stress-free.

We feel calm. No more pressure.

Maybe we could start by saying, "Would you like to hear an option?"

And if they say "yes," then our conversation will be easy and enjoyable.

When we offer our business and services as an option, prospects notice this. No prospect is forced to buy just because we talked to them. Everything we offer is an option.

An option means, "It is okay if I take advantage of this, or not. No one is going to pressure me either way." This feels very safe for prospects. They relax, and they have no reason to reject us.

To avoid feeling nervous, simply remember the word, "option."

But it gets better!

Here is the best news of all.

Most people are pre-sold on what we have to offer. That means we don't have to sell.

No selling. If our prospects already want what we have, all we have to do is avoid talking too much. We don't want to talk people out of it.

If this seems hard to believe, let's take a survey. We will go out and ask 100 people, "Do you like to save money, or do you like spending too much?" Almost everyone wants to save money. They are pre-sold on our services.

Next, we will ask 100 people, "Do you want more money in your life, or less money?" Most people want extra money. They want to hear more from us.

Wow!

So here is our new approach.

1. Prospects want what we have to offer.

2. Don't be a sleazy salesman and try to convince them.

3. Instead, give them the option of our services and opportunity.

4. Let them choose if now is a good time for them to say "yes."

That wasn't so hard, was it?

Now, let's move on to the four steps of conversation we will use when we talk to our prospects. Remember them?

Step #1: Rapport.

Step #2: Ice breaker.

Step #3: Closing.

Step #4: Presentation.

Step #1: Build rapport first.

Rapport means that our prospects trust us and believe us.

Without rapport, our message fails.

Think about it this way. If our prospects don't trust us, will they ever join our business? Of course not. And if our prospects don't believe us, will they ever buy our services? Of course not. Without trust and rapport, we waste our time. Our message will bounce off our prospects' foreheads, never once entering their brains. Their skepticism wins. We lose.

Rapport is different from relationships. We can create trust and belief in a few seconds. Relationships? Well, those take a lot longer. We don't have to worry about deep relationship-building now. All we have to do is to create enough trust and belief to deliver our message.

This decision to trust and believe only takes seconds?

Yes. Prospects prejudge us harshly in the first few seconds. Humans make quick decisions. Why?

Thousands of years ago, a caveman would meet a stranger. He must make a quick decision. Will this stranger be helpful? Or will this stranger be dangerous? If the caveman spends too much time thinking it over, it could be fatal.

What about today? When a stranger walks through the door, we instantly prejudge the stranger. Will it be okay if the stranger sits next to me? Should I guard my wallet or purse? Why is this stranger wearing a hockey mask and carrying a chainsaw? Yes, we still make snap decisions based upon a few seconds' worth of information.

Our first challenge in network marketing is to build good rapport with our prospects.

But first, some good news. We already have rapport with most of the people we know. Unless we stole their bicycle, or ran over their pet, most people will trust and believe what we say.

Strangers? We don't have rapport with these people. We will have to be conscious in our efforts to build rapport with them. But, this only takes a few seconds.

The first few seconds we invest in building rapport are the most important part of our conversation. We have to have rapport before we deliver our message.

What happens if we don't build rapport? Here is what our prospects will think:

- "What's the catch?"
- "I don't know you."
- "You sound like a salesman. I need to be careful."
- "What is your agenda?"
- "It's too good to be true."

When our prospects have these thoughts, they protect themselves by creating objections to keep us away. What do these objections sound like?

- "I am not interested."

- "I am too busy."

- "I need to think it over."

- "It is not for me."

- "I am happy with my current situation. No new ideas, please."

Ready, set, go.

How do we build rapport in the first few seconds?

By letting people know that we think the same way they do. If we see the world from the same viewpoint, we will make the same decisions. That feels safe. That is why we are more comfortable with people who are more like us than people who are different than us.

How do we emphasize our similarities?

By telling our prospects a fact that they believe and we believe. Yes, starting with one little fact that we have in common helps create belief and trust. Starting with disagreement is a bad plan. That creates skepticism.

We want a library of facts to choose from so we are ready for any situation with any prospect. Here are some good opening lines and facts that we can use for utility services:

- Things are so expensive these days.

- Electricity rates keep going up and up.

- Everyone wants lower bills.

- It is so expensive to live here now.

- We get mobile phone bills every month.

- Saving money is important.

- Everybody loves a bargain.

- Getting an instant discount makes sense.

- Nobody wants to be paying the highest rate on their street.

These facts are safe. They also introduce our business into a social conversation. This is a great way to both be in agreement with our prospects and to move our conversation forward.

Some facts about our business opportunity?

- Commuting to work gets harder and harder.

- We would love to spend more time with our children.

- It would be great to pay for the holidays with cash instead of credit cards.

- Jobs take up a lot of time.

- Two paychecks are better than one.

- It is difficult to get a pay raise now.

- We wish weekends were longer.

- We dream about firing the boss.

A good way of looking at this is that starting with agreement is good manners. People like people who think like they do. Our bonus is that we will see our prospects' heads nodding as we speak. This is a great feeling.

Make it better.

How? Double the facts. When we tell our prospects two true facts in a row, their brains say, "I can trust you."

Now that we have our prospects' trust, it will be easier to talk about our business. Here are some examples of putting two facts together:

- "Things are expensive now. We all need more money."
- "Of course we need electricity. But wow, they charge so much!"
- "We get our mobile phone bills every month. It would be nice if they were lower."
- "Jobs interfere with our week. It would be nice to have three-day weekends forever."
- "It is hard to get a raise now. But, prices keep going up and up."
- "Having our own business sounds great. However, we have to be careful not to take too much risk."

All we are doing is assuring our prospects that we see the world the same way they do. This makes them more comfortable in dealing with us.

What happens when we start with disagreement?

Our prospects build a wall that shuts out our message. No matter how good our message or offering is, our prospects won't hear it.

We want our prospects in an open, positive state of mind. Then we can deliver our message. Once our message is inside their heads, they can decide if our message will serve them or not. That means we don't have to use any power-closing techniques.

All we have to do is deliver our good message inside their heads without a lot of baggage or prejudice.

The decision to trust us or not happens quickly.

We have to be fast. Those first few seconds make the difference. So what can we do to enhance our chances of rapport?

Use magic words. Certain words and phrases help our prospects make a decision to agree with us. Let's start with "most people."

Here is what happens when we say, "Most people."

Our prospects think, "Am I part of most people, or am I part of less people? Well, most people are part of most people, so I must be in that group. Plus I enjoy being part of most people. It feels safe. That is why I choose a crowded restaurant instead of an empty restaurant. That is why I want to walk through a dark alley late at night with a group of people instead of alone."

Notice how this feels when we say:

- "Most people like saving money."
- "Most people want to save on their bills."
- "Most people want more money."
- "Most people would rather work from their homes."
- "Most people want something better."

By using "most people," our phrases are easier to trust and believe. But this isn't the only magic word phrase we could use. Let's look at the phrase, "Everybody knows."

Some examples?

- "Everybody knows we offer better service."
- "Everybody knows it will be hard to get pay raises this year."
- "Everybody knows home businesses get great tax deductions."
- "Everybody knows that rates will continue to go up."
- "Everybody knows that if we work hard, only our boss gets a big house when he retires."
- "Everybody knows we don't get paid enough."
- "Everybody knows that if we don't do something different now, then tomorrow will be a repeat of today."

Or, we could use the phrase, "Everybody says." These words have the same effect as "everybody knows." Our prospects will want to agree with what we say. It is easier to take the path of least resistance.

A word about smiling.

It works.

Our natural tendency is to trust people who smile, and to distrust people who don't smile. It doesn't take a rocket scientist to figure out that we should smile when we meet new prospects.

Babies react to smiles before they can talk. If we smile as we walk down a street, many people will react and smile back.

If we think being extremely serious works, we won't have many prospects buying or joining.

Remember, our prospects make their initial decision to trust and believe us within a few seconds. A smile on our faces helps them feel more comfortable with us. We want to do everything possible to keep our prospects' minds open so that they hear our good message.

What if we don't have a natural smile? Now is the time to practice. Let's not allow our non-smiling face to keep prospects from trusting us. We want to be professionals. That means putting everything in our favor to deliver our message to our prospects' minds.

Do compliments work?

Direct compliments sometimes feel insincere. We make our prospects uncomfortable. Some examples of direct compliments?

- "Hi, what a beautiful house."
- "You seem like a smart consumer."
- "You are looking sharp today."

Compliments like these don't feel right. They appear too obvious and seem shallow.

What is a better way to make a compliment?

Focus on something a bit less obvious, and then add a question. When we add a question at the end of our compliment, our prospects don't have to acknowledge it and thank us. Instead, they focus on answering our question. This is more comfortable for everyone. Some examples?

- "I like your phone. How did you go about choosing that model?"
- "I see you like saving money by collecting coupons. Where did you learn that?"

- "Your children are so polite. How did you get them to be that way?"

So yes, compliments do work. But adding a question at the end makes everyone feel better about them.

STEP #2: ICE BREAKERS.

Q. What is the definition of an ice breaker?

A. A short sentence that introduces our business into a social conversation in a socially acceptable way.

We can't keep our business a secret forever. At some point we will have to let our prospects know what we're offering. We meet many prospects in social situations. That means we should be careful how we bring our business into that conversation.

Ever feel so excited about our business that we forget about our prospects' feelings? We want to tell our prospects everything about our business. But do they want to know everything? Of course not. Here is what is socially acceptable and considered good manners.

Give our prospects an option to hear more, or to change the conversation.

Ever been in this situation? Someone jumps into a sales presentation that we don't want to hear. They talk and talk because they are excited. We are not. It is torture.

We don't want to be that person.

Instead, our ice breaker will introduce our business. Then we will pause, giving our prospects a chance to say, "Tell me more." Or, after the pause they can change the subject because they have no interest in what we are saying. Being polite works.

Why is this pause important? Because prospects want choices. Prospects have limited time. And prospects have a lot on their minds. In the next moment, our prospects will make a decision. They will choose to know more, or they will choose to move on to the next item on their list.

Does this seem cruel? It isn't. We also have many things to think about during our day. We choose where to focus our time also.

Here is our strategy. We will make our ice breaker so powerful that our prospects beg us for more information.

Think about this. If our prospects beg us for more information, what decision have they made? They are making a "yes" decision to what we offer. This means we won't even have to close at the end of our conversation.

Our ice breaker is so important to getting that final "yes" decision. And this all happens in the first few seconds of our conversation. Closing doesn't happen at the end of our conversation. Prospects make a decision early and quickly. They have other things to think about that are waiting for their time.

Rapport first.

We took the time to build rapport. Now our prospects trust and believe what we say. This is the perfect time to introduce our business.

But do our prospects care about us? No.

It gets worse. They care even less about what we have to offer.

What do prospects care about?

Themselves. The world revolves around them. When we introduce our business with ice breakers, we want to focus on our prospects, not on us and our business. Our ice breakers will be all about our prospects' points of view.

Our ice breakers will look selfish and socially awkward if they are about us. Some examples of bad ice breakers?

Us at a funeral, talking to the widow: "I am so sorry about your husband's death. But have you checked how much you are paying per kilowatt hour on your electricity bill?"

Okay, slightly exaggerated, but we get the point. We need to have more concern about our prospects' situations.

Consider this scenario. We are at a party. Everyone at the party looks like a great prospect for us. They have electricity. They have phones. They could use an extra income. We just can't wait to talk to them, but how do we start the conversation?

Us: "What is your name?"

Prospect: "My name is Ann."

Us: "Ann. Your name starts with the letter 'A.' My company starts with the letter 'A.' Let me tell you about my company now."

Yes, this seems forced, because it was all about us. We forgot to focus on our prospects and their needs.

And did we notice that we didn't pause? We wanted to go right into our presentation. We didn't give our prospect a chance to opt out of it.

Now, let's improve our ice breaker technique.

Commanding our prospects' attention.

It is easy to get someone's attention. All we have to say is, "I just found out."

What is the other person thinking? The other person might wonder, "What did you find out? Is it something I need to know? Will this be important to me?"

Those four simple words, "I just found out," not only grab our prospects' attention, but also give us a chance to introduce our business. Here are some examples of using these words for our ice breakers.

- "I just found out how we can lower our electricity bill."
- "I just found out how we can get paid every time our neighbors turn on their lights."
- "I just found out how we can reduce our mobile phone bill to zero."
- "I just found out how we can save on our utility bills."
- "I just found out how we can get an extra paycheck."
- "I just found out how we can work out of our homes instead of commuting to a job."
- "I just found out how we can go into business together, and do it part-time."

We can almost feel the "yes" answer after we make our "I just found out" statement. Closing feels automatic.

And we know our prospects want what we offer when they reply, "Tell me more. How does that work?"

Why does this works so well?

#1. We only continue talking to prospects who are interested. They asked us for a presentation. No pressure from us.

#2. We don't set off any salesman alarms. We make a statement. Prospects can volunteer their interest by asking us to tell them more.

#3. This approach is 100% rejection-free. There is nothing holding us back from talking to prospects.

It feels good when we don't have to pressure our prospects, doesn't it?

Want to make this completely safe and easy?

All we have to do is continue the conversation on a different topic after we announce what we "just found out." How does this sound?

- "I just found out how we can get an extra paycheck. If you would ever like to know how, I would be glad to tell you. Meanwhile, let's ask your cousin to join us tonight at the event."

- "I just found out how we can save on our electricity bill every month. If you would ever like to know how, I would be glad to tell you. Meanwhile, let's go shopping."

- "I just found out how we can save big on our mobile phone bills. If you'd ever like to know how, I would be glad to tell you. Meanwhile, tell me how you got this recipe."

Because we continue the conversation on a different topic, our prospects don't have to comment on our announcement. They can ask us for more details if they are interested. Or they can ignore our ice breaker if they have no interest.

This means we will only have conversations about our business with people who want to know more.

What happens when we try to force the conversation to continue about our business? If our prospects don't want to hear more, they are afraid to say, "I made a decision that I am not interested. And I made this decision even before I heard what it is." That would sound silly. So what do they do? They make up phantom objections. Here are some examples of phantom objections they use to keep us from continuing with a presentation.

- "I am not a salesman."
- "I don't have any time."
- "It is a pyramid."
- "This is not for me."

As we can see, prospects use these objections to protect themselves from unwanted presentations.

We won't have to worry about these objections anymore. We will only talk to the volunteers.

Ice breakers are fun.

And they are so easy to do. The first step is to make a list of our benefits. We will want benefits for our opportunity and for our services. Let's start a list right now.

Benefits for our services.

- Save money on our electricity bill.
- Save money on our mobile phone bill.
- Get our energy for free.
- Get all our services on one bill.

Benefits for our opportunity.

- Never show up for work again.
- Work from home instead of commuting.
- Retire 10 years early at full pay.
- Double our pension in only nine months.
- Get two paychecks instead of one.
- Fire our boss.
- Work three weeks out of the month but get paid for four.
- Take a one-week holiday every month.
- Take a six-month holiday twice a year.
- Have a monthly income to pay off our student loans.
- Earn more money part-time than our boss does full-time.

Okay, these are some benefits to start with. All we have to do is start our ice breaker with the words, "I just found out." Then, add an appropriate benefit for our prospects. Now we know why those previous examples felt so good to use.

If our ice breaker resonates with our prospects, they will make a mental "yes" decision and ask us to tell them more.

No stress. No selling. No ugly social mistakes.

If we are observant, we can customize our benefit to fit our prospect. This is what professionals do. So take a moment to have empathy for our prospect.

For example, imagine we talk to a retail clerk during the weekend. We could say, "I just found out how to never have to work weekends again." That could be a huge motivation for this retail clerk.

Another example of observing? Imagine we have a conversation while waiting to pay for our groceries. The other person has a handful of coupons ready so she can save money on her purchase. Easy. We say, "I see you use coupons and like to save money. I just found out how we can save on our utility bills also."

Our prospects make quick decisions based upon the words we use. This is why some networkers have all the prospects they need, while others struggle. When we say the wrong words, no one wants to volunteer. So instead of blaming prospects for being unmotivated, we should change the words we say.

Here is a little conversation that helps us remember that we influence the outcome by saying better words.

Distributor: "My prospects weren't interested."

Us: "Weren't interested in what?"

Distributor: "Weren't interested in what I said."

Us: "Then, stop blaming the prospects ... and change what you say."

Distributor: "Well, how can I be a professional victim if you keep talking to me like this?"

It is all over in seconds.

In the first few seconds, our prospects sort us out and make their decisions. That is why we have to be effective during these first few seconds.

So instead of spending hours practicing our long presentation, we should memorize great benefits that will interest our prospects. Now our job is not to convince prospects. Our job is to mention our benefits and allow prospects to volunteer.

No selling. No high-pressure closing. No stress.

Is this the only opening for an ice breaker?

No.

For variety, we can use many other opening phrases. Let's look at another phrase that gets our message into a social conversation.

"Would you like to know more?"

We mention a benefit, and ask our prospects if they would like to know more. If they do, we are glad to give them more details.

This is permission-based prospecting.

Good manners.

Being polite reduces rejection. We want to give our prospects a chance to opt out of our prospecting conversation. No one likes pushy salespeople.

What are some phrases we could use to make our prospecting conversations easier?

- "Would you like to know more?"

- "Would you like to know how I am doing it?"

- "Would you like to hear how they did it?"

Our bonus for using these phrases early in our conversations?

When prospects say they want to know more, they make a "yes" decision. Prospects know if they want something or not.

Humans love to do this. We want to make a "yes" or "no" decision quickly.

Then, if the answer is "yes," we welcome a presentation and more information.

Most problems come when we push sales presentations on prospects. Avoid this grief with simple little questions, such as:

- "Would you like to know more?"

- "Would you like to know how I am doing it?"

- "Would you like to hear how they did it?"

"Why do people hate to sell?"

Because they believe selling is like what they see in the movies. In Hollywood, an aggressive, ethically-challenged actor plays the role of the salesman, who forces people to buy against their will. Okay, maybe this is what happened in the 1970s, but the 1970s are not coming back.

The old model of selling? Make cold calls. Lots of cold calls. Pitch anyone and everyone who will listen. And, if we can get an appointment, dump everything we know about our opportunity or service on the prospect. Sell, sell, sell.

After we beat our glazed-eyed prospects into submission, then we go for the close. We use trial closes, hard closes, any close that could shame our prospects into buying. And if they don't buy immediately? Then we follow up. We harass our prospects until they buy or die.

Does that sound like fun? Of course not. Nobody wants to sell that way. Yet many people today still use the old way of selling.

This is not how prospects buy anyway. It is out of sync with the buying process. Would we like to be sold this way? This is not how we buy, is it?

This explains our reluctance to make calls, our fear of prospects, and why people don't want to join our business.

Here is the short story.

Prospects want to know the big picture first. They can immediately make a "yes" or "no" decision, based upon the current programs in their mind. If the answer is "yes," then and only then should we begin a presentation.

If this seems reasonable, that our prospects make their final decision within the first 20 seconds, then we are in sync with how our prospects love to buy. No more presentations until our prospects make a "yes" decision.

Want an example of this more humane way of talking to prospects using, "Would you like to know more?"

Distributor: "I help families get an extra paycheck. Would you like to know more?"

Prospect: "Yes. Tell me more."

Our business is simple when we don't have to hard-sell prospects. This feels right.

A few more examples.

> Distributor: "I am getting a big reduction in my electricity bill. Would you like to know how I am doing it?
>
> Prospect: "Yes. Tell me more."
>
> Distributor: "I went online and saved a lot on my electricity bill. Would you like to know what I did?"
>
> Prospect: "Yes. Tell me more."

Now, did that feel comfortable for our prospects? Comfortable for us also? Yes!

> Distributor: "My neighbor saves an extra $30 on his mobile bill every month. Would you like to know how he is doing it?"
>
> Prospect: "Yes. Tell me more."

No one gets offended by this kind of conversation. And even if we were talking to cold prospects, they would want to know more details also.

> Distributor: "I am paying off all my credit cards by the end of this year. Would you like to know how I am doing it?
>
> Prospect: "Yes. Tell me more."
>
> Distributor: "My friend finally got rid of his job, and now works from home. Would you like to know how he did it?"
>
> Prospect: "Yes. Tell me more."

Distributor: "I started a small part-time business. It only gives me 20% of my salary, but it also means I only have to work four days a week now. Would you like to know how I did it?"

Prospect: "Yes. Tell me more."

We could use this technique anywhere. Networking events. Family reunions. Idle conversations during coffee breaks at work.

This is the safest way to introduce our business to prospects. When prospects can volunteer to know more, they feel open-minded and positive about what we will say next.

Want to be a little more professional?

Yes, we can guess which benefits would help our prospects. But there is a better way.

Listen for hints.

Allow our prospects to tell us exactly the problems they have in their lives. All we have to do is sort through these problems and find one that we can help with. Now our ice breakers precisely target the problems and concerns of our prospects.

The result? We look like a mind-reader.

1. Our prospect has a problem.

2. We have a great solution.

3. Allow our prospect to decide if now is a good time to fix their problem.

An example?

Prospect: "I hate commuting downtown every day. It takes over an hour each way."

Us: "My friend, John, stopped commuting last year. He now works out of his home. Would you like to know how he did it?"

Prospect: "Tell me more!"

Or,

Prospect: "It is hard to get by with things being so expensive."

Us: "I just found out how we can save some money on our regular utility bills. Would you like to know how others are doing it?"

Prospect: "Tell me more!"

Sometimes, this business feels so easy.

STEP #3: CLOSING.

Step #1: We build rapport. Our prospects trust us and believe us.

Step #2: Our ice breaker creates interest. Our prospects instantly decide if these benefits will work for them or not.

At the end of step #2, if our prospects ask for more details, they want what we have to offer.

Will 100% of our prospects want what we have to offer immediately? No. Maybe they had a fight with their spouse 30 minutes before they talked with us. We can't control our prospects' timing. However, we can control the words we say. This gives us our best chance to get a customer or a new distributor.

A good way to look at closing is that our prospects now have a chance to take advantage of our message, or not. What a relief! We don't have to look like some sleazy used-car salesman from the movies.

At the end of step #2, our prospects have options. They could say:

- "That sounds great. Let's do it. Give me the details now." (Yes!)

- "That sounds great. I have other pending issues now." (This is not for me right now.)

- "Did you see the football game on television last night?" (This is not for me.)

We are not in charge of our prospects' lives. They are. They must live with their decisions and the subsequent consequences. We deliver a great message, and the rest is up to them.

Some prospects might say, "I want to continue paying more for my electricity bill. I don't want to change." Their choice. Not our choice. Not everyone makes sensible decisions for their lives. They probably have other problems too. We don't have the psychology qualifications to deal with all of their problems.

Remember, our job is to deliver a great message. That is it.

So we just let closing ... happen?

Yes. We appreciate the same courtesy in our lives. We appreciate the option of a salesperson honoring our choices.

But don't prospects need more information to make up their minds?

Choices come first. Information comes later.

Prospects don't need information if they've made a "no" decision. That would waste their time and our time.

How long will it take prospects to decide if they want to save money on their utility bill or not? That choice should take seconds.

How long will it take prospects to decide if they want an extra paycheck in their lives or not? That choice should take seconds.

If our prospects make a "yes" decision, then we can move forward and give them any information they want.

Does this seem strange? Here is an example.

At the end of a meeting, we say to the attendees, "By a show of hands, who wants to come with me to get ice cream when we finish?" Most attendees will make an instant "yes" or "no" decision. Maybe half of the attendees raise their hands. Decision made.

The decision for ice cream came **before** we said where the ice cream parlor is, what flavors of ice cream are available, how much saturated fat would be in each scoop of ice cream, etc. Some of the attendees who raised their hands will have a few questions about this. Other attendees can't wait to leave for ice cream.

It is the same process with our prospects. The simple decision to save money, or to have more income every month, takes about one second.

We ask our prospects to decide if they want our benefits or not. The details can come later.

No pressure.

We effectively give our prospects an escape plan. They won't feel trapped by a salesman with a single-minded agenda. Prospects relax when they feel that they are in charge of their choices, and that we are not there to argue with them.

When our prospects make their "yes" decision, how do we move forward? How do we make sure that now is the right time to proceed safely?

If we feel shy about closing, or if we want to get permission to continue, here are a few phrases that might feel comfortable:

- "Let's get that sorted."
- "Let's fix that now."

These phrases make it easy for our prospects to move forward with us ... now.

How would we use these phrases? Here is an example.

Us: "I just found out how we can save some money on our regular utility bills."

Prospect: "That sounds great! That is something I need."

Us: "Let's fix that now."

Prospect: "Uh, what do you mean?"

Us: "Get me a copy of your electricity bill and I will get it sorted."

Prospect: "Oh. Good idea."

When prospects want what we have, the conversation is fun.

Will every conversation be this easy? No.

There are many reasons why a prospect would not be interested in talking to us right now. Maybe:

- They are busy.
- They don't need what we have to offer.
- Their interests are elsewhere today.

Let's be polite.

Allow our prospects an opportunity to say "no" and we save everyone time.

And that is it? Yes.

Short. Simple. Done.

A NEW DISTRIBUTOR MAKES IT EASY.

I had dinner with a new distributor who sold electricity. He said, "My new business is amazing! It is so easy."

Why? Here is what he told me.

"In the last 2 months, all I did was ask these two questions.

"1. Do you get an electricity bill?

"2. Would it be okay if it was lower?

"I added 35 personal customers. And I was thinking, 'Customers are easy to get. Maybe I should build a team also.'

"Getting new team members was easy. I just told my friends, 'If you can memorize two questions and take the volunteers, you can have a great part-time income.'

"Training my new team is simple. I help them memorize and practice these two questions:

"1. Do you get an electricity bill?

"2. Would it be okay if it was lower?

"I love my new business!"

Let's review.

This new distributor's ice breaker?

"Do you get an electricity bill?"

Great ice breaker. Not pushy. Introduces our business into a social conversation.

This new distributor's close?

"Would it be okay if it was lower?"

No pressure. Just needs a "yes" or "no" answer. If the answer is "yes," then we could put their decision into action by saying, "Let's fix that now."

Prospects prefer simple choices. They don't have time for reviewing complicated plans, weighing five different options, and reviewing industry data and statistics. Long presentations may interest a few people, but the majority want clear, quick choices. Then they can get on with their lives.

If prospects prefer simple, we should deliver simple. If they need more information in any one area, they will gladly ask. Short is always better than long.

Want to add a bit more to this short conversation?

Try saying this:

***

"When you go shopping, do you pay regular price or do you try to find bargains and discounts?"

"Then you will love this."

"Do you get an electricity bill?"

"Would it be okay if it was lower?"

"Let's get that sorted now."

***

These five sentences won't take long to memorize.

Let's see what is happening sentence by sentence.

"When you go shopping, do you pay regular price or do you try to find bargains and discounts?"

The first sentence commits our prospects to taking discounts. The majority of people don't want to pay full price. When prospects make a verbal commitment, they want to be consistent. No one wants to say, "No. I changed my mind. I like paying more."

Once our prospects make a commitment to discounts, we win.

If we don't do this, here is what happens. At the end of our conversation, our prospects might say, "No. I don't think so. I won't save enough money to make changing worthwhile. I will stay where I am."

At the end of our first sentence, we should know if we will have a customer or not.

Here is what is even better. This sentence is totally noninvasive. Any new team member will feel comfortable asking this question several times a day!

What a great way to prospect for customers with no rejection.

"Then you will love this."

Here is what happens when we say, "Then you will love this." Our prospects take a positive frame of mind. In a way, we commanded them to love what we are going to say next. How good is that?

"Do you get an electricity bill?"

Of course our prospects will say, "Yes." But think about this from our new team members' point of view. Getting "yes" responses from their prospects gives them confidence. When they feel good, it shows. People like doing business with people who are confident.

"Would it be okay if it was lower?"

Another "yes" answer from our prospects. Not only do our team members feel more confident, they also close their prospect immediately. Their prospects committed to wanting to save money. No more stress. The decision has been made.

"Let's get that sorted now."

This moves the sale forward and puts everyone into action now. These words sound confident. Most prospects follow our suggestion to get their electricity bills lowered immediately.

Using proven phrases makes building our business quick and easy.

Network marketing professional Cesar Rincon is a master of these short, proven phrases. In a few words, he gets his prospects interested, qualified, and closed.

Compare his skill with brand-new distributors. They randomly talk and hope prospects figure things out for themselves. This is a bad plan. Prospects don't have time for us to be unprofessional. We have to be like Cesar Rincon. He gets to the point. He makes it clear.

Step #4: Presentation.

Our prospects say, "Sounds pretty good. But I need to know more."

Now is the time for our presentation. The decision has been made. Now it is a matter of details. But how many details?

Let's listen closely to exactly what our prospect said. He said, "I need to know more." He didn't say, "Please tell me everything you've ever learned about your business."

Time to be polite. We don't want to tell people more than they want to know. It is rude, a waste of their time, and might even talk them out of it.

More people talk themselves out of the sale than listen their way out of the sale. It is better to say too little than to say too much. If we say too little, they can ask for more.

In past years, salesmen believed that sales presentations convinced prospects to make decisions. There was a lot of pressure to create elaborate presentations with graphics, videos, PowerPoint and endless proof and testimonials.

Now, we know that was wrong.

Decisions happen before the presentation begins.

We don't need a sales presentation to convince prospects to want what they already want. That means all the pressure is off us, and our prospects. Now our presentations can be a relaxed conversation where we answer our prospects' questions, and help them understand the details.

No convincing during our presentation. No agenda during our presentation.

For some prospects, all they may want to know is the name of the company. For others, they may want to know every detail about our business. Not everyone will want the same amount of information.

So how do we know how much information our prospects might want?

Here are some possibilities:

- Micro-presentation. Give a three- or four-sentence micro-presentation that summarizes the big picture. Then, wait for our prospects to ask for more details.

- Give a one-minute presentation. Then, wait for our prospects to ask for more details.

- Tell a two-minute story. Then, wait for our prospects to ask for more details.

- Ask an individual prospect, "What would you like to know first?" Then, continue answering questions as they arise.

Notice that none of the above options include, "Tell our prospects everything we know. Read the PowerPoint presentation to them as if they are reading-impaired. Bore prospects with one-size-fits-all corporate commercial videos. And tell prospects to quietly sit and save their questions until the end, while we talk **at** them about our wonderful company and services."

When we first start our business, we haven't learned a lot of presentation options. We don't know much about our business.

Our confidence may not be at peak levels. In that case, we will default to a presentation that has a lower chance of success.

That would be sending our prospects away to look at a website or a corporate video. Then we hope our prospects will magically get excited, and come back to us begging to join. It could happen, but not often. But in the beginning, this might be our only option.

But we can get better.

Why should we improve our skills? So that we can treat our prospects like people, not some generic number that we send away to watch a pre-packaged sales pitch. We want to honor our prospects as real people with real needs. This is the power of person-to-person network marketing.

If all it took was sending out millions of messages to watch a video, our companies wouldn't need us. They could do this themselves. Our person-to-person conversation gives us a huge advantage over some corporate advertisement.

Which presentation do you think is more powerful?

1. Our mother sees a video online that asks her to switch her telephone service. Or,

2. We personally ask our mother to switch her telephone service.

Which offer has more weight? The second one, of course. Big corporations would love to have the person-to-person advantage that we have.

As soon as possible, we are going to need to learn some sort of presentation. So let's start with a small three- or four-sentence micro-presentation that gives our prospects the big picture. This might be all they need. Or if they would like to learn more, they can ask more questions based upon what we just presented.

Micro-presentations (the big picture).

This is an easy way to start.

Give a three- or four-sentence micro-presentation that summarizes the big picture for our prospects. Once they hear the big picture, they have some choices.

1. "That is all I need to know. Let's get started."

2. "Could you tell me a bit more about this point?"

3. "I would like to see a long, formal presentation."

We follow the path our prospects want. Nothing complicated. They appreciate that we are there to help them.

Here is an example of a business micro-presentation if we sold mobile phone service.

"We don't sell. Everybody has mobile phone service already. We can give them a lower monthly bill. They are happy and we get paid."

That is a clear message. Our prospects "get it" without having to listen to a lot of fluff or hype.

Will our prospects appreciate this big-picture view? Yes! Because now we pause.

This pause allows prospects to ask for an additional explanation on anything we said. There is nothing worse than prospects having questions but no chance to ask them. That creates unnecessary tension in our prospects. We hate it when sales-people give a monologue with no pauses. We feel frustrated because we want to ask a question. We don't want to be one of those non-stop salespeople.

Let's look at this micro-presentation for our services.

"Everybody gets an electricity bill. We go online and show them how to make it smaller. They love us. And most end up telling their friends about it also."

Now our prospects are thinking, "I should tell my friends to talk to you also. They will appreciate a chance to save money."

Big tip: It is easier to get referrals by including that last sentence, "And most end up telling their friends about it also."

Two more examples.

"People can keep their high bill, or spend five minutes online making their bill lower every month. I can help you go online to do this."

"Save on your monthly utility bills. Let your neighbors do the same. Get your utilities for free."

Nothing scary about these presentations. Shouldn't take very long to learn.

But what about our business opportunity?

That is more complicated. Can we do a micro-presentation for this also?

Of course. We don't have to explain every detail. All we do is give the big picture. Our prospects can decide which part of the big picture they want to know more about. Or, they could appreciate that our big picture got to the point, and they feel comfortable.

If we like, we can add a few extra sentences, but always keep it short. Here are some examples.

"You will save on your electricity bill. Let your neighbors know that they can save also. They will love you. You get paid every time they turn on their lights."

"Be a hero. Let your friends and neighbors know they can stop overpaying for their utilities. Help them go online to set up a better rate. Get a paycheck for helping them."

"Want your own business helping people save some money on their mobile phone bills? Start part-time out of your home. Build your business to a full-time income."

"Want a career helping people? Feel good every day when you help others save money on their utilities. The more people you help, the more you earn."

"Have big dreams? Build a business network of part-timers who help their friends and neighbors save money. The bigger your network, the bigger your paycheck."

"Everyone gets an electricity bill. Help one person a day arrange to get a lower bill. In six months, you might be able to replace your full-time income. No more commuting."

Obviously these are abbreviated versions of our opportunity. This big-picture overview allows our prospects to relax and feel comfortable with what we offer. There will be plenty of time to talk about the company background and the finer details of the compensation plan after our prospect relaxes.

When we are clear about the big picture, skepticism goes away. We present the facts as an option for our prospects' lives. Our prospects can make their choices for their lives.

Will this short overview be enough for most prospects? Probably not. But it does relax them and help them figure out which questions they would like to ask. It is much better to be in a conversation than in a sales presentation.

Let's jump ahead and do a more structured short presentation.

THE ONE-MINUTE PRESENTATION.

Give a 30-minute presentation, and we will hear objections such as:

- "Oh. I need to think it over."
- "I couldn't do this. Memorizing 30 minutes would be impossible."
- "Can I get back to you later? I need to do something right now."
- "I don't have any time now. I can't take on another project."
- "I don't know anyone. I seldom go out."
- "Looks like you have to be a salesman. This is not for me."
- "I don't know how to do this. I wouldn't be any good at it."
- "My spouse and I don't do these sorts of things."

Are these real objections? No.

Our prospects are being polite and telling us "no" without rejecting us personally.

What went wrong? Our prospects couldn't see themselves talking to their friends and relatives like we did to them. This is a clue. We should present to our prospects in a way that feels more comfortable for them.

Getting more appointments.

The one-minute presentation makes it easy to get appointments. We don't have to call someone and ask them for 30 minutes or an hour of their time. Instead, we ask permission for a short one-minute presentation. For our prospects, it is easier for them to grant us permission than to try and avoid us.

All we need to do is memorize two friendly sentences. Here they are:

> 1. "I can give you a complete presentation, but it would take an entire minute."

The second sentence is:

> 2. "When could you set aside a whole minute?"

What will most people will say?

"Go ahead. I am curious about this. Tell me now."

Our prospects will be listening. We will not be fighting through sales filters or salesman alarms. They will look forward to our one-minute explanation.

We could use these two sentences over the phone. Sometimes our prospects don't want to invest 30 minutes or an hour in a meeting. They want the big picture now. Why? Because they value their time.

To protect their time, they are looking for something they don't want. That means they can get off the conversation right away. They won't have to invest their valuable time listening to details about something that is not a good fit for them.

When we deliver the big picture to these skeptical prospects, they feel good. Because we did not withhold information from them, they don't react with skepticism and sales resistance. Now they are more open-minded.

It gets better.

Our "big picture" is more structured in the one-minute presentation. We want to answer our prospects' three pressing questions:

1. What kind of business are you in?

2. How much money can I make?

3. Exactly what do I have to do to earn that money?

It won't take long to answer these three questions.

If we answer these three questions clearly, our prospects can then tell us:

1. "Yes, I want to join."

2. "No, I don't want to join."

3. "I have a question or two."

Here is a quick generic example of a one-minute presentation that takes less than 15 seconds:

"You can become a stuntman for movie productions. You can earn $100,000 a year. And all you have to do is risk your life daily doing stupid stunts others don't want to do."

Our prospects received the answers to their three basic questions:

1. "What kind of business are you in?" (You can become a stuntman for movie productions.)

2. "How much money can I earn?" (You can earn $100,000 a year.)

3. "Exactly what do I have to do to earn that money?" (And all you have to do is risk your life daily doing stupid stunts that other people don't want to do.)

Clear. Simple. And enough of a presentation that most people can make their decision.

Let's look at how we could answer these three questions for our utility business.

Question #1: "What kind of business are you in?"

This is not a good time to be vague or try to sound important. This is a great time to be clear and to the point. We want our prospects to understand.

Our prospects don't want to know about our business yet. They first want to know what kind of business it is. Why? Because no one would ever join a business if they didn't know what kind of business it was. Or maybe our prospect has a prejudice against certain types of businesses. Now is a good time to find out.

Here are some possible ways of answering that first question.

"We are in the mobile phone business. Everyone uses mobile phones."

"We are in the electricity business. Most people in our neighborhoods use electricity every day."

This simple explanation lets our prospects know what we do. If we find that this explanation is not clear enough, we can add a bit more. The easiest transition words are "which means." Here is an example:

> "We are in the electricity business, which means when people get their normal electricity bill, we help them make it smaller."

The long explanation and details will be saved for only those prospects who are interested.

Question #2: "How much money can I make?"

This is a great place to use our common sense and listening skills. If our prospects do not give us a hint about how much money they want to earn, we could guess.

Or, to be more accurate, we could ask them.

Someone looking to change careers will want to know how to make a lot of money. Others may only want a part-time income to help with the family budget.

How would this sound in real life?

To start off our one-minute presentation, we could say, "If you wanted to earn an extra $500, you would have to do these three things."

Yes, we would start our one-minute presentation by immediately telling our prospects a monthly figure they could earn. No need to hold them in suspense. Prospects love us when we get to the point.

As we continue our one-minute presentation, our prospect can now focus on our explanation of our business. But at the end of our presentation, we will again remind our prospect of the monthly amount.

We could end by saying, "And then you would earn an extra $500 a month."

Don't worry about this now. We will give a complete one-minute presentation in a moment so we can see how everything fits in.

Question #3:
"Exactly what do I have to do to earn this money?"

This is where the magic happens. This is the burning question all prospects have.

Of course our answer to this question will depend on what our prospects want to earn. So, we will do a few examples.

All of these examples are approximations. At this point in the conversation, our prospects don't want to know every rule about qualifying for certain bonus levels. Our prospects don't want 22 different examples. What do they want?

A rough overview of the activity they would have to do to earn this amount of money.

Here is what they don't want to hear:

"Just talk to people."

"Share our message with your friends."

These answers are too vague. We will give them one example. Will this one example be 100% accurate 100% of the time? No. In every compensation plan, you can arrange team members in different configurations, earn different bonuses, add or subtract fast-start bonuses from the total, etc. The purpose of this example is only to answer, "What do I have to do to earn this money?"

We are answering the "activity question," not the details of the compensation plan. So it is okay to leave out some information at this moment. We can cover that later if they are interested.

The key is to make this clear and short. Some examples:

"Spend two evenings a week helping people reduce their mobile phone bills. At the end of six months, you will be earning $500 extra a month."

"Every week, help one family save money on their mobile phone bill. And of all the people you help, eventually find four people who want a part-time income doing the same thing. And at the end of one year, you will be earning an extra thousand dollars a month."

"Find four people who hate their jobs and want a bigger opportunity in their lives. Help each of them get their first 50 customers, and then you will be earning an extra $2000 a month."

Now, are any of these examples 100% accurate for your business? Of course not. They could be higher or lower depending on your compensation plan, fast-start bonuses, special promotions, if your new team members sponsored other team members, etc.

All of those comparisons can be made later in training. For now, our prospects only want to know, "Generally, what type of activity will I be doing to earn this money?" We will be polite and answer this pressing question in their minds.

Let's put all three steps together.

Our prospects tell us, "Yes. I have one minute. Tell me about the business." Our answer?

> "We are in the mobile phone business. Everyone uses mobile phones. You can earn $500 extra a month. All you have to do is spend two evenings a week helping families reduce their mobile phone bill. At the end of six months, you will be earning $500 extra a month."

Wow. That takes less than 20 seconds.

Is this everything our prospects want to know? No.

However, this is all they want to know right now. This gives them a chance to make an initial "yes" or "no" decision without investing a lot of their time. If this sounds interesting to them, we can explain all the details next.

In time, we will learn to do this more elegantly. But for now, this will be sufficient for most people that we will be talking to.

Notice what we left out.

We didn't talk about:

- How utilities deliver their services.
- When utilities were discovered.
- The background of the company's leader.

- The different steps in the compensation plan.
- Where we can set up the PowerPoint presentation.
- Our company's commercial videos.
- The size of the utility market.

In less than 15 seconds, our prospects have the big picture. They can give us a "no" decision right away, and we will still be friends. We don't have to avoid each other in the future.

Our prospects can also say, "I think this is great. Sign me up."

And if our prospects want more details, they can ask. We will do our best to answer the questions as clearly as possible.

This one-minute presentation works face-to-face and on a phone or video call. No more misleading invitations to secret meetings. Our prospects can relax by knowing what to expect.

Now, let's see how this one-minute presentation might sound in real life.

Us: "I can give you a complete presentation, but it would take an entire minute. When could you set aside a whole minute?"

Prospect: "Right now. Go ahead."

Our presentation:

"If you want to earn an extra $500 a month, you would have to do these three things."

(When we say three things, our prospect feels that we are getting directly to the point, no long sales pitch. And three things don't sound that intimidating either.)

"Number one: Don't change. Continue recommending things you like." (Our prospect feels comfortable. It is natural for humans to recommend things we like to others. This also tells our prospect that he will stay within his comfort zone.)

"Number two: We are in the electricity business. Everyone gets an electricity bill monthly. We simply spend a few minutes with them to help them get a bigger discount." (Our prospect understands our business. This is clear.)

"And number three: All you have to do is spend two evenings a week helping families get a discount on their electricity bills. At the end of six months, you will be earning $500 extra a month." (Our prospect knows this will take two evenings away from television, and won't expect to earn $500 a month right away.)

Done!

Finished!

Over!

Now we give our prospects a chance to speak. There is nothing worse than us talking too long. When we stop speaking, our prospects have a choice. We just wait for our prospects to make the choice that serves them best at this moment in their lives.

Some people fear change. They will insist on paying more. That is okay. That makes them happy.

Other people welcome a discount. They will insist on changing immediately. They feel every second wasted is money out of their pockets. We can help them change now.

When we visit with prospects, they have no obligation to buy or join. We simply offer our services or business as an option for their lives.

Let's do one more example.

"If you want to earn an extra $500 a month, you would have to do these three things.

"Number one: Don't change. Continue to recommend things that you like, such as your favorite music or favorite movie.

"Number two: We are in the telecommunications business, which means we help people save a fortune on their mobile phone monthly charges.

"Number three: All you have to do is help one person join your team every month, and help them get their first four happy customers to kickstart their business.

"And then, at the end of eight months, you would earn an extra $500 a month."

When we are clear, our prospects relax and hear our message.

But what if our prospects don't make an immediate decision?

"Thinking it over" is the same as making a "no" decision. "Thinking it over" is a decision to not change. It is okay if our prospects consciously make a decision to stay where they are.

We just want to make sure they are aware that "thinking it over" means they are turning down savings, or turning down the opportunity for more money in their lives.

Here is a simple closing statement that helps prospects understand that they will either make a decision to change, or make a decision to stay where they are. Here it is:

"This either works for you, or not. So what do you want to do?"

Some examples?

"Saving money on your mobile phone bill every month either works for you, or not. So what do you want to do?"

"Getting a discount on your electricity bill every month either works for you, or not. So what do you want to do?"

"Having an extra $500 a month in your family's budget either works for you, or not. So what do you want to do?"

"Building a part-time business in your spare time so that you can quit your job next year either works for you, or not. So what do you want to do?"

"Having a career where you can work out of your home either works for you, or not. So what do you want to do?"

"Making your electricity bill smaller by going online for five minutes either works for you, or not. So what do you want to do?"

This basic closing statement helps prospects focus on what they want for their lives. When we ask this question, they don't feel pressured. Instead, they relax because now they know they are in charge of their choices for their lives.

Don't stress.

Our ice breaker pre-closed our prospects. The hard work of closing is already over. Our presentation is the easiest part.

Plus, if we keep our presentation short, our prospects will feel great. Our prospects believe that a bad one-minute presentation is always better than a perfect 30-minute presentation. Prospects prefer talking rather than listening to us anyway.

And here is an added bonus. This presentation is so short that our prospects think, "I can do this business. This explanation is so easy."

Can we improve our presentation skills from here? Of course.

If we are brand-new, these short presentations are a good place to start. They will give us confidence and prevent us from talking too long. In the next chapter, let's look at a more advanced presentation for our business opportunity.

THE TWO-MINUTE STORY.

This presentation works when we talk to an individual prospect.

It is not appropriate for a group meeting. Why? Because we will have a conversation with our prospect. We need to get feedback from our prospect so that we can customize this presentation to our prospect's needs.

It is not appropriate for selling our services. The story is about our opportunity. And it is not appropriate for someone looking for a small part-time income.

This story only works well for someone looking for a career change.

Yes, this story has limits. But it makes it easy for prospects to see themselves succeeding in a full-time network marketing career.

Margaret Millar once said, "Most conversations are simply monologues delivered in the presence of a witness." And that is the problem with standard presentations. All the communication is one-way. We end up preaching to our prospects.

The two-minute story changes this. Instead of giving a one-size-fits-all memorized presentation, we create a story in our prospects' minds configured to their current situation. Prospects love it when we talk about them.

But let's get to work now on an actual two-minute story. It is easier to demonstrate than to explain.

The invitation.

How do you think our prospects would respond if we said the following?

"I've got a good story."

Most prospects would say, "Great, tell me the story." Why? Because humans love stories.

Whenever someone tells a story, our mind says, "Stop. Listen to the story. It may be important for our survival." Also, a story is more interesting than presentations and facts. We love movies and books because they tell stories.

Even children love stories. From the moment they can talk, they say, "Mommy, Daddy, tell me a story." Not only do we get our prospects' interest, we get their favorable interest. That is important. They will hear what we have to say.

Let's continue the invitation.

"I've got a good story. Takes about two minutes. Might make you a lot of money, might not. Do you want to hear it?"

What do you think our prospects will say? "Yes!"

Think about this from our prospects' points of view. What do they like about this invitation?

- "I've got a good story." Prospects love listening to stories.

- "Takes about two minutes." Prospects love listening to short stories, not long stories.

- "Might make you a lot of money, might not." The promise of money? This sounds very interesting.

- "Do you want to hear it?" We give our prospects an option of opting into further conversations. No pressure. They can volunteer.

This simple invitation to the "two-minute story" gets our prospects to volunteer to hear our short presentation.

Here it is again. This is something we should memorize word-for-word, and have it ready to say at any moment:

"I've got a good story. Takes about two minutes. Might make you a lot of money, might not. Do you want to hear it?"

What's next?

We will start our story with a question. This will help us personalize this story.

"Would it be okay if you never had to show up for work again?"

Our prospects think, "What would that look like to me? Could I stay home and play my guitar and work on my music? Maybe I could homeschool my children and be with them as they grow up? Will this be my chance to travel to the places of my dreams? Let me imagine what it would feel like to sleep in late every morning."

Our prospects will create the perfect vision in their minds. At this moment our prospects create a dream of what their lives could be. If our prospects don't have dreams, there will be no motivation for them to start.

This is better than us guessing what our prospects' dreams could be. Some people want to travel. Others want to pursue their passions. We don't know. So instead of guessing, let's allow our prospects to create their perfect visions.

Here is our second sentence:

"So how much money would you need a month, just to cover the basic bills, so that you would never have to show up at work?"

Is this too personal? No. We didn't ask how much money they currently earn. In most societies that would be rude. Instead, we only wanted to know the minimum amount they would need to take care of their current bills. This will be the minimum amount they need to avoid showing up for work every day.

Notice we did **not** ask how much money they would **like** to earn. That number could be huge. We want to keep the amount as low as possible. Then it is easier to show how our opportunity can help them reach this goal. Imagine this number as just enough to pay the bills and have a few pizzas delivered to the house every month.

Now that we have this number, we're done with our information-collecting process. Let's see what our presentation looks like so far.

∗∗∗

"I've got a good story. Takes about two minutes. Might make you a lot of money, might not. Want to hear it?"

"Would it be okay if you never had to go to work again?"

"So how much money would you need a month, just to cover the basic bills, so that you would never have to show up at work?"

∗∗∗

Assuming is better than selling.

Instead of selling the benefits of our service, we will assume that we have an awesome value for our prospects. When we assume with confidence, our prospects naturally believe us. Why else would we be so confident?

We are not technically selling our prospects on our services at this moment. We just want our prospects to know that others will buy and use our services. We want to establish that there is a market for what we have to offer. No one wants to join a business where no one will buy.

Here is the sentence that we will use:

"Well, you know how most people get an electricity bill?"

When we start with "Well, you know how," our prospects begin nodding "yes" immediately. Then, we say a fact that our prospects will agree with. "Most people get an electricity bill" is a great fact to use. Who could argue with that?

What happens? At this moment our prospects agree that many people will be using our services. We accomplish our mission.

But what if we sell mobile phone service? This example is about electricity, but we could substitute anything. Use your imagination.

Our next sentence will tell our prospects a little bit about our company. We can insert a small sales plug for our business here.

"There is a company called [our company] that shows people how to get their discount, so they can save money on their monthly electricity bill."

Our prospects will assume that our company is good, and helps consumers save money on their electricity bills. They should be thinking, "Everyone would want this."

Just a few sentences so far. Here they are.

***

"I've got a good story. Takes about two minutes. Might make you a lot of money, might not. Want to hear it?"

"Would it be okay if you never had to go to work again?"

"So how much money would you need a month, just to cover the basic bills, so that you would never have to show up at work?"

"Well, you know how most people get an electricity bill?"

"There is a company called [our company] that shows people how to get their discount, so they can save money on their monthly electricity bill."

***

So far, so good. Our prospects are nodding "yes" and are on our side. No tension. No selling. No pressure.

But back to our story's continuation.

We have the details out of the way. Our prospect knows what we do in our business. We also know how much money our prospect needs to cover his minimum expenses, so that he doesn't have to go to work.

Now, let's get back to the original question we asked: "Would it be okay if you never had to go to work again?" Our prospect might be wondering when are we going to tell him how he can stay home instead of going to work.

So, let's continue. We will say:

"Now, if you wanted to never go to work again, all you would have to do is help 400 families save money on their electricity bills."

Let's explain this sentence. We started our sentence by saying, "Now, if you wanted to never go to work again." We start with this phrase to refocus our prospect on the original question. We don't want our prospect thinking about something else at this time.

Then we say, "All you have to do is." This signals to our prospect that our explanation will be concise and easy to understand. Prospects love this.

And finally, we have to explain the compensation plan. At this point in the conversation, our prospect doesn't want to know the details of the compensation plan. Our prospect wants to know, "Generally, what would I have to do to earn this money so that I can stay home?"

Our prospect does not understand our network marketing terminology. We can't use words such as "legs" or "levels" or "group volume." We have to communicate our explanation in terms our prospect can understand immediately.

So how do prospects understand business? They visualize a small shop with customers. They measure a business by its customers. So, we will use the customer explanation.

The last part of our sentence will be, "Help 400 families save money on their electricity bill." This is clear and easy to understand for any prospect.

But there is a problem. Our prospect will panic and think, "400 families! I don't know 400 families. That is impossible!"

Don't worry. We will take care of this fear in the next sentence.

But how did we arrive at 400 families? It is an approximation. We know roughly how much is earned on each customer. But, it changes depending on if we found that customer personally, if our team found the customer, if there was some sort of fast-start bonus or promotion at that time, etc. Plus, we adjust the number of customers based upon how much income our prospect needs to stay home and cover his bills. Someone who needs $5000 a month will need a lot more customers.

Don't worry about the exact number. We just want to pick something close so that our prospect understands our business.

Overcoming our prospect's panic attack.

Our prospect thinks, "400 customers! That is too many. I could never do that."

To relax our prospect, we will do a mind-reading trick. Yes, we will read our prospect's mind. We will say:

"Now, you don't know how to get 400 customers, but you can learn. You learned how to use a smartphone, you learned how to use that 100-button remote control for your television, and you certainly can learn a system to help 400 customers save money on their electricity."

Wow! Now what is our prospect thinking?

"Oh, you are so right. I don't know how to get 400 customers. You read my mind. I can trust you. And I did learn how to use my smartphone. And that remote control? That was tough, but I learned. I could be borderline genius. I have the ability to learn new things. Now, they say they have a system. I like how that sounds.

I can get step-by-step instructions that I can learn and follow. While this sounds difficult now, their system will train me to get 400 customers. So, I think I can learn their system and do this."

This one sentence does a lot of work. At the end of the sentence, our prospect sees the possibility of our business replacing his full-time income at work.

Won't this sentence bring up a lot of questions from our prospect?

Possibly. Some prospects can have lots of questions.

The good news is that we don't have to be experts to answer these questions. Most of the questions can be answered by saying, "You will learn how to do that when you learn our system."

Here are some examples.

Prospects: "I don't know where to find people who want to save on their electricity."

Us: "Don't worry. You will learn how to do that when you learn our system."

Prospects: "I don't know how to talk to people."

Us: "Don't worry. You will learn how to talk to people when you learn our system."

Prospects: "I am a shy person. I am not comfortable talking to strangers."

Us: "Don't worry. You will learn how to be very comfortable with others when you learn our system."

Prospects: "I don't know how to do this or any business."

Us: "Don't worry. The company doesn't expect us to know how to do this business before we start. That is why we have training. You will learn how to do this business step-by-step when you learn our system."

We will answer our prospects' questions by referring to the "system." This will give our prospects confidence that they can successfully build their business.

Before we explain all the details of our system, we first need to get a decision from our prospect. There is no need to go through all the details of our training with someone if they are not going to join. That would waste a lot of time.

But, before we close, let's see how our two-minute story looks so far.

***

"I've got a good story. Takes about two minutes. Might make you a lot of money, might not. Want to hear it?"

"Would it be okay if you never had to go to work again?"

"So how much money would you need a month, just to cover the basic bills, so that you would never have to show up at work?"

"Well, you know how most people get an electricity bill?"

"There is a company called [our company] that shows people how to get their discount, so they can save money on their monthly electricity bill."

"Now, if you wanted to never go to work again, all you would have to do is help 400 families to save money on their electricity bills."

"Now, you don't know how to get 400 customers, but you can learn. You learned how to use a smartphone, you learned how to use that 100-button remote control for your television, and you certainly can learn a system to help 400 customers save money on their electricity."

***

Our "two-minute story" is looking great! So let's get the "yes" or "no" decision from our prospect.

How to wrap it up and get the decision.

To do this, we will ask a simple question. We want to know if our prospect wants to stay where he is, keep his life the same ... or if our prospect wants to go into business with us.

That is it. That is the only decision we need at this point.

If our prospect gives us a "no" decision, and prefers to keep his life the same, that is okay. We are done. Our prospect will still remember this story. So when times are difficult in the future, our prospect will think of us, and think of us fondly. Timing is everything.

How do we ask this closing question? Here it is.

"So what is going to be easier for you?"

What a nice question. No pressure on our prospect. We look great also. We don't look like some pushy salesman with an agenda. All we do is ask our prospect if he wishes to keep his life the same, or join with us. We leave our prospect in control of his life and his choices.

How do we do this? We continue our question with two choices.

Choice #1: Keep your life as it is. Don't change anything.

Choice #2: Change your life. Start your new business now.

Here are some examples.

"So what is going to be easier for you? To continue struggling with one paycheck? Or to start learning a system for your new business so that you never have to show up for work again?"

"So what is going to be easier for you? To continue waking up at 6 AM every morning to fight traffic to work? Or, to learn a system so that you can have your own business and work out of your home?"

"So what is going to be easier for you? To continue going to the job you hate five days a week? Or to start your business with us tonight, so maybe next year you can work out of your home?"

"So what is going to be easier for you? To continue letting other people raise your children at daycare? Or, to start your business this evening so that maybe next year you can be home with the children?" (Okay, a bit strong and exaggerated. But, it is easy to remember.)

"So what is going to be easier for you? To hope for a 50% pay raise at work? Or, to enroll in training now and learn the system, so that you never have to show up at work again?"

"So what is going to be easier for you? To work a part-time job for the rest of your life to make ends meet? Or to start tonight, create a part-time business to help with monthly expenses, and build it to a full-time business quickly?"

And then we are done.

Our prospects can choose which option will be easier for them. They choose the option, and we have no need for closing. We respect our prospect's choice.

Let's take a look at this two-minute story in its entirety.

The whole story.

Ready?

This is the story that can change our lives.

***

"I've got a good story. Takes about two minutes. Might make you a lot of money, might not. Want to hear it?"

"Would it be okay if you never had to go to work again?"

"So how much money would you need a month, just to cover the basic bills, so that you would never have to show up at work?"

"Well, you know how most people get an electricity bill?"

"There is a company called [our company] that shows people how to get their discount, so they can save money on their monthly electricity bill."

"Now, if you wanted to never go to work again, all you would have to do is help 400 families to save money on their electricity bills."

"Now, you don't know how to get 400 customers, but you can learn. You learned how to use a smartphone, you learned how to use that 100-button remote control for your television, and you certainly can learn a system to help 400 customers save money on their electricity."

"So what is going to be easier for you? To continue struggling with one paycheck? Or to start learning a system for your new business so that you never have to show up for work again?"

***

If this story could make us financially free, how much effort should we put into learning it?

Yes, it is a bit more complicated than a four- or five-sentence presentation, but it is worth it.

And if this story could make presenting effortless for us and our prospects, how often would we use it? It certainly makes phone conversations shorter.

Ask network marketing professional Jerry Scribner, who is one of the best at using the two-minute story to build his business. Everything we need to do is over in less than two minutes. No more long initial presentations only to find out our prospects aren't interested.

Prospects love the two-minute story. Think about this from their viewpoint. It is all about them, and it is short and to the point.

Once we tell the story for a few weeks, we can repeat this story in our sleep. Instead of worrying what comes next in the story, we can then focus on our prospects and how we can help them.

The two-minute story is the most powerful business opportunity presentation we can give one-on-one with a prospect. We customize the story to our prospect's income needs. The story is all about our prospect. It is the most interesting story in the world.

GROUP PRESENTATIONS.

Ever feel nervous in front of a group?

Relax. This is normal. Why do we feel nervous?

Because the entire group is judging us. That would make anyone nervous!

When we stand up in front of a group, here is what others are thinking. "Who are you? Will you be interesting? Is this going to be a sales pitch? How long is this going to last? Should I believe you? Let me check out your sense of fashion."

Our group is not thinking about our business opportunity. They are too busy judging us.

Take control of their minds immediately.

Humans can have only one thought at a time. Let's put another thought in their minds so they won't have room for all these negative thoughts about us. How will we engage their minds?

We can start with a question. Now the group has to think about their answers to our question. Their minds are off us, and on to answering the question. Problem solved.

After our initial question, we can continue challenging their minds. That way they will focus on what we present to them.

And here is the good news.

We only have to control their minds for the first 30 seconds. After 30 seconds, our group will make their decisions. So we want to get our entire message compressed into the first 30 seconds. Anyone can learn and memorize 30 seconds about their business. Want to see this in action?

We will come to the front of the group, and say this.

***

"Here is the short story. How many people here this evening get a mobile phone bill? Ask yourself, 'Would it be okay if my mobile phone bill was lower and I could spend my savings on things I enjoy?' That is what we do. Now, ask yourself, 'Would my neighbors love me more if I allowed them to save money just like I do?' Of course they will. By doing this, you will earn money every time your neighbors use their mobile phones."

***

Notice that we did not talk **at** our prospects. We had a conversation with them. A pleasant conversation.

Our conversation was so engaging, our prospects didn't have time to think about us or judge us. Did you notice how we kept our prospects' minds engaged?

This entire opening to our group presentation took only 30 seconds. Most prospects will be thinking at the end of our 30 seconds, "Yeah. This makes sense. Sounds pretty good to me."

We spoke clearly, and our proposition was easy to understand. Nothing stressful for our prospects' minds. At this point, our prospects are on our side. Now they welcome the details we are about to show them.

Prospects will want details only after they make a "yes" decision. Prospects don't want to waste their time. They only want time-consuming details on things that interest them.

Let's see why this works so well. We will analyze each sentence.

"Here is the short story." (This opening sentence relaxes our prospects. They worry if we will talk too long. This sentence announces to them that we will get to the point, and not steal their time with some boring, long-winded presentation.)

"How many people here this evening get a mobile phone bill?" (Our prospects now consider this question in their minds. They think, "Sure. I get that bill." And now they forget about us. They are thinking about themselves and their bills.)

"Ask yourself, 'Would it be okay if my mobile phone bill was lower and I could spend my savings on things I enjoy?'" (We have our prospects talking to themselves about our business. This question is a no-brainer. We know our prospects will say "yes" to this question.)

"That is what we do." (Clear and to the point. Our prospects love what we do. How good is that?)

"Now, ask yourself, 'Would my neighbors love me more if I allowed them to save money just like I do?'" (Their minds picture their neighbors. No time to be thinking about us.)

"Of course they will." (They can visualize themselves being thanked by their neighbors.)

"By doing this, you will earn money every time your neighbors use their mobile phones." (Nothing else to discuss. We told the whole story in 30 seconds.)

Our first 30 seconds handled the decision. Everything past this point will be small details. We can relax.

We are only 30 seconds away from having a great group presentation about our business opportunity. It is what we say first that will make the difference. This is why we concentrate so hard on the first 30 seconds.

But what about a group presentation for potential customers?

Here is a different approach. We can start with our personal story, and our potential customers will see themselves in the same situation. They will visualize our story in their minds, but with themselves as the main characters. And guess what? They will come to the same conclusion that we did.

Here is our story to start the group presentation.

"I hated bills. Just the thought of opening those bills stressed me out. High mobile phone bills, but my family needs the phones. High electricity bills that kept going up and up, but no one can live without electricity. The first thing I did was go online and get discounts on my bills. Next, I told 15 other people to do the same. Now, my bills are free. I smile every time they show up in the mail."

Then we ask the group, "How do you feel about your electricity bill every time it comes in the mail?"

Our prospects will naturally make the same decision that we did. Having free bills make sense.

But what if we don't offer discounts or free bills for referrals? Then, we can describe our personal savings. The group will see that in their minds also.

Group presentations are fun and easy to do. When we make the first 30 seconds awesome, the rest of the presentation is easy.

And a bit of humor to end this chapter on group presentations.

Q. The best way to get people to sit in the front row at opportunity meetings?

A. Provide power outlets to charge their mobile phones.

Okay, one more.

Q. Are you afraid of the dark?

A. Wait until you see your summer electricity bill.

WHERE AND HOW TO FIND PROSPECTS.

We now have the skills to give short presentations. With a question or two, we can qualify our prospects. A few sentences are all we need to get our prospects to make "yes" decisions.

The good news is that our friends and relatives will enjoy our non-sales approach.

The bad news is that we will run out of people that we know quickly.

Where do we go from here? How do we find new prospects? Let's go to work.

Prejudging.

It sounds like a bad word, but it is something we do.

Not everyone is a prospect. People who live in Mongolia? Not prospects. People who are ill-tempered and hard to talk to? Not prospects. People younger than 18? Not prospects. As we can see, not everyone is a prospect for our business.

But, there are a lot of people left. Too many people for us to talk to. Our time is limited. So who should we choose to talk to? People who are open-minded and looking for what we have to offer? Or people who are too difficult or barely qualified?

The answer is obvious. It we can only talk to one segment of this large group, let's talk to the most qualified people. We want to talk to those who have the best chance of becoming customers or business partners.

Imagine this. Every person knows at least 200 people who we don't. We don't want to talk to all 200 people. Many fail to qualify. But out of the 200 people someone knows, there must be five or ten people who would be perfect for our business and our services. Let's spend our time talking to these prospects.

How do we find them? Ask.

We can ask our current customers. We can ask our friends who did not join. And, we can ask complete strangers if they know people who want what we have to offer.

Here is the wrong way to ask for these referrals: "Do you know anyone that would be interested?" Most people will reply, "No." We won't get many referrals this way.

How can we ask for referrals in a rejection-free way? We will use this little script instead:

"I am curious. Can you do me a favor? I am looking for people with this problem, who want to fix it. Do you know anyone like that?"

This script will give us a better chance for referrals. Let's break this down sentence by sentence.

- "I am curious." There is something about this phrase that disarms people. It even makes mean people nice. These are great words to start a conversation with a stranger.

- "Can you do me a favor?" Most people are glad to do us a favor if it does not cost them money or obligate them to move our furniture.

- "I am looking for people with this problem, who want to fix it." We tell them the type of person we are looking for. This person has a problem. But we also qualify this by making sure they want to fix their problem. No use talking to them if they don't want to fix their problem.

- "Do you know anyone like that?" If we seem trustworthy, they will give us the name of someone who needs our help.

So what is the "problem" in this little script? It is a problem that we can solve. Let's see this in action.

"I am just curious. Could you do me a favor? I am looking for people with electricity bills, who want to lower their bills this summer. Do you know anyone like that?"

What was the problem? Getting an electricity bill every month is a problem. And in summer, people use more electricity. Their bills get higher. Now we will get a referral of someone who wants a lower bill. This will be easy.

How about this?

"I am just curious. Could you do me a favor? I am looking for families with two or more mobile phones, who want to lower their total bill. Do you know anyone like that?"

This is the key sentence. "I am looking for people with this problem, who want to fix it." All we need to do is change this sentence in this little script, and we can have all the referrals we need.

Some examples of this key sentence for our business opportunity?

- I am looking for stressed single moms, who want to change their lives.

- I am looking for people with jobs, who want to be free.

- I am looking for college students with debt, who want a way to pay off their loans quickly.

- I am looking for people who are tired of commuting, and would rather work out of their homes.

- I am looking for people about to retire, who want to double their pension.

- I am looking for people with lots of credit card debt, who want a way of paying it off quickly.

- I am looking for people with low-paying careers who would like to earn a lot more.

- I am looking for people stuck in low-wage jobs, who want to earn a lot more.

- I am looking for people who like to travel, but would like to win free trips instead of spending their own money.

- I am looking for parents with jobs, who want more flexible hours so that they can be home with the children.

- I am looking for people who love coffee breaks and chatting with people, and would love to have a career taking five coffee breaks a day.

In 15 minutes, we could create a huge list of possible things we could say.

Here is my favorite one.

"I am looking for people with two jobs, who would like to get rid of one of those jobs."

What do we know about people with two jobs? Well, they need extra money. That is why they are working. They are self-starters. They went out and got that extra job. Do they want to work two jobs for the rest of their lives? Of course not. If we could help them get rid of one of their jobs, they would be thrilled. We could expect a big hug. And if we could help them get rid of both of their jobs, they might hug us so hard it would crush our ribs.

This little prospecting script can point us towards the best, most open-minded prospects who other people know. So if we have a choice of who to talk to, let's talk to the most qualified people we can.

Finding good prospects to talk to is easy. So many people have problems, and we have solutions.

What to say at networking events.

Business breakfast clubs, local Chamber of Commerce mixers, lead-swapping groups, MeetUp groups, and more. There is no shortage of places where prospects get together. Here is an excerpt from our book, *51 Ways and Places to Sponsor New Distributors.*

***

Many years ago, Bob and Anna Bassett from Canada shared their "Five-Question Test." They told me the story of their friend, Herbie.

Herbie would be talking to a prospect at a networking event, and then suddenly, turn and walk away, sometimes in mid-sentence. When asked about the abrupt behavior, Herbie answered:

"Well, he didn't pass the Five-Question Test."

What's the Five-Question Test?

Herbie explained, "Well, when I meet somebody new, I try to learn as much as I can about him by asking questions. I ask him five questions during our conversation, and if he hasn't asked me anything, then I know he is only interested in himself. I just walk away. There is no point in talking to anyone who doesn't pass the Five-Question Test."

Prospecting isn't all about you. It is all about the prospects.

Don't start by talking all about you and your company. Soon no one will be listening. Instead, learn as much as you can about your prospects.

Find out if they have a problem you can solve. Build a relationship with them. Then, when they decide to solve their problem, they will choose to solve it with you.

It doesn't matter if your prospects pass the Five-Question Test. What matters is that **you** pass the Five-Question Test.

***

So how do we find out if our prospect has a problem? We ask.

Prospects love to talk. They will have no problem answering our questions. In fact, they appreciate our interest in them.

Now, our prospect will be doing most of the talking. We listen. We pick up hints about our prospect's problems. When we hear a problem that we can solve, we will ask a question or make a comment about that problem. Sometimes we have to wait a bit before we get a chance to ask or comment.

Here are some examples of what our part of the conversation might sound like.

"Are you okay with being so busy you don't have time for your family?"

"How do you feel during that long commute every day?"

"Do you expect a huge raise at work this year?"

"Yeah. Jobs don't give us any hope. If we don't start our own business, then we are sentenced to a lifetime of labor."

"You are right. Things are so expensive now. What are you doing to save money on your bills?"

"Yeah. When we add up all the mobile phone bills of our families, we could buy a small car."

We could use this same technique at parties.

If we don't like to go to outside networking events, we can go to parties!

Help the host. Grab a tray of appetizers, and go guest-to-guest, offering them something to nibble on. What an easy way to start the conversation. It won't take us long to find an appropriate time to say our ice breaker.

How many parties can we go to? Oh my! This could be a fun challenge.

With unlimited pre-sold prospects to choose from, prospecting won't be a problem.

AND FINALLY.

All the techniques in this book work better when we use them. Having knowledge and not using it is the same as not having the knowledge.

So let's review the big picture.

Most prospects we meet are pre-sold. They want to save money. They want more money in their lives.

We should talk to prospects in these four steps, keeping them in the correct order.

Build some rapport first.

Introduce our business with an ice breaker.

Close our prospects. Get their decision now.

And finally, if our prospects' answer is "yes," give them a presentation.

If we keep these steps in the correct order, we won't have to worry about rejection. Our prospects will love us.

And this makes our network marketing business not only fun, but profitable.

And as Chris and Debbie Atkinson say, "It's never too late." We can change our lives starting ... now.

Thank you.

Thank you for purchasing and reading this book. We hope you found some ideas that will work for you.

Before you go, would it be okay if we asked a small favor? Would you take just one minute and leave a sentence or two reviewing this book online? Your review can help others choose what they will read next. It would be greatly appreciated by many fellow readers.

I travel the world 240+ days each year.
Let me know if you want me to stop in your
area and conduct a live Big Al training.

BigAlSeminars.com

FREE Big Al Training Audios
Magic Words for Prospecting
plus Free eBook and the Big Al Report!

BigAlBooks.com/free

MORE BIG AL BOOKS

10 Shortcuts Into Our Prospects' Minds

Get network marketing decisions fast! We only have a few seconds before our prospects make their decisions. Use these seconds wisely.

How to Get Your Prospect's Attention and Keep It!
Magic Phrases for Network Marketing

Getting attention is the easy part. Keeping that attention requires using these magic phrases to ward off distractions.

Mini-Scripts for the Four Color Personalities
How to Talk to our Network Marketing Prospects

As network marketing leaders, we want to move people to take positive actions. Using their own color language is how we will do it.

Quick Start Guide for Network Marketing
Get Started FAST, Rejection-FREE!

Our new team members are at the peak of their enthusiasm now. Let's give them the fast-start skills to kick-start their business immediately.

The Two-Minute Story for Network Marketing
Create the Big-Picture Story That Sticks!

Worried about presenting your business opportunity to prospects? Here is the solution. The two-minute story is the ultimate presentation to network marketing prospects.

How to Meet New People Guidebook
Overcome Fear and Connect Now

Meeting new people is easy when we can read their minds. Discover how strangers automatically size us up in seconds, using three basic standards.

How to Build Your Network Marketing Business in 15 Minutes a Day

Anyone can set aside 15 minutes a day to start building their financial freedom. Of course we would like to have more time, but in just 15 minutes we can change our lives forever.

How To Get Kids To Say Yes!
Using the Secret Four Color Languages to Get Kids to Listen

Turn discipline and frustration into instant cooperation. Kids love to say "yes" when they hear their own color-coded language.

Why Are My Goals Not Working?
Color Personalities for Network Marketing Success

Setting goals that work for us is easy when we have guidelines and a checklist.

Closing for Network Marketing
Getting Prospects Across The Finish Line

Here are 46 years' worth of our best closes. All of these closes are kind and comfortable for prospects, and rejection-free for us.

Pre-Closing for Network Marketing
"Yes" Decisions Before The Presentation

Instead of selling to customers with facts, features and benefits, let's talk to prospects in a way they like. We can now get that "yes" decision first, so the rest of our presentation will be easy.

The One-Minute Presentation
Explain Your Network Marketing Business Like A Pro

Learn to make your business grow with this efficient, focused business presentation technique.

Retail Sales for Network Marketers
How to Get New Customers for Your MLM Business

Learn how to position your retail sales so people are happy to buy. Don't know where to find customers for your products and services? Learn how to market to people who want what you offer.

Getting "Yes" Decisions
What insurance agents and financial advisors can say to clients

In the new world of instant decisions, we need to master the words and phrases to successfully move our potential clients to lifelong clients. Easy ... when we can read their minds and service their needs immediately.

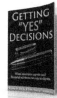

3 Easy Habits For Network Marketing
Automate Your MLM Success

Use these habits to create a powerful stream of activity in your network marketing business.

Start SuperNetworking!
5 Simple Steps to Creating Your Own Personal Networking Group

Start your own personal networking group and have new, pre-sold customers and prospects come to you.

The Four Color Personalities for MLM
The Secret Language for Network Marketing

Learn the skill to quickly recognize the four personalities and how to use magic words to translate your message.

Ice Breakers!
How To Get Any Prospect To Beg You For A Presentation

Create unlimited Ice Breakers on-demand. Your distributors will no longer be afraid of prospecting, instead, they will love prospecting.

How To Get Instant Trust, Belief, Influence and Rapport!
13 Ways To Create Open Minds By Talking To The Subconscious Mind

Learn how the pros get instant rapport and cooperation with even the coldest prospects. The #1 skill every new distributor needs.

First Sentences for Network Marketing
How To Quickly Get Prospects On Your Side

Attract more prospects and give more presentations with great first sentences that work.

Motivation. Action. Results.
How Network Marketing Leaders Move Their Teams

Learn the motivational values and triggers our team members have, and learn to use them wisely. By balancing internal motivation and external motivation methods, we can be more effective motivators.

How To Build Network Marketing Leaders
Volume One: Step-By-Step Creation Of MLM Professionals

This book will give you the step-by-step activities to actually create leaders.

How To Build Network Marketing Leaders
Volume Two: Activities And Lessons For MLM Leaders

You will find many ways to change people's viewpoints, to change their beliefs, and to reprogram their actions.

The Complete Three-Book Network Marketing Leadership Series
Series includes: How To Build Network Marketing Leaders Volume One, How To Build Network Marketing Leaders Volume Two, and Motivation. Action. Results.

51 Ways and Places to Sponsor New Distributors
Discover Hot Prospects For Your Network Marketing Business

Learn the best places to find motivated people to build your team and your customer base.

How To Prospect, Sell And Build Your Network Marketing Business With Stories

If you want to communicate effectively, add your stories to deliver your message.

26 Instant Marketing Ideas To Build Your Network Marketing Business

176 pages of amazing marketing lessons and case studies to get more prospects for your business immediately.

Big Al's MLM Sponsoring Magic
How To Build A Network Marketing Team Quickly

This book shows the beginner exactly what to do, exactly what to say, and does it through the eyes of a brand-new distributor.

Public Speaking Magic
Success and Confidence in the First 20 Seconds

By using any of the three major openings in this book, we can confidently start our speeches and presentations without fear.

Worthless Sponsor Jokes
Network Marketing Humor

Here is a collection of worthless sponsor jokes from 25 years of the "Big Al Report." Network marketing can be enjoyable, and we can have fun making jokes along the way.

ABOUT THE AUTHORS

Keith Schreiter has 20+ years of experience in network marketing and MLM. He shows network marketers how to use simple systems to build a stable and growing business.

So, do you need more prospects? Do you need your prospects to commit instead of stalling? Want to know how to engage and keep your group active? If these are the types of skills you would like to master, you will enjoy his "how-to" style.

Keith speaks and trains in the U.S., Canada, and Europe.

Tom "Big Al" Schreiter has 40+ years of experience in network marketing and MLM. As the author of the original "Big Al" training books in the late '70s, he has continued to speak in over 80 countries on using the exact words and phrases to get prospects to open up their minds and say "YES."

His passion is marketing ideas, marketing campaigns, and how to speak to the subconscious mind in simplified, practical ways. He is always looking for case studies of incredible marketing campaigns that give usable lessons.

As the author of numerous audio trainings, Tom is a favorite speaker at company conventions and regional events.

Made in the USA
Middletown, DE
24 April 2020